poems written by a late b

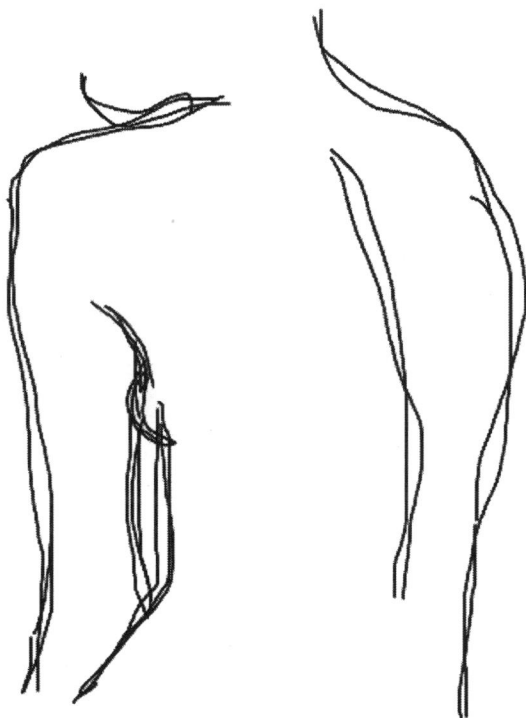

written and illustrated by karli crispin

table of contents

summary

this collection of poetry
explores the complex feelings
around trauma depression sexuality
love friendship and healing
i have sometimes wished
people could read the thoughts
that enter my mind
because they are the truest part of me
sometimes these thoughts represent the best in me
but they can also represent the worst
and i am going to share both with you
because humans are not all good or all bad
we overwhelmingly live in the gray area
and this is what makes the human experience
so frustratingly beautiful

dedication

for my sister
who gives me the world
just by breathing

i love you

disclaimer

this book does contain references to suicide, molestation, and sexual assault

i know that these can all be very triggering subjects so i have listed what subjects will be mentioned on what page

there will be a trigger warning on the previous page as well

i hope drawing light to these sensitive topics can help us have difficult and honest conversations with each other

and to anyone who is struggling

i hope this book can help you feel less alone in some of your struggles.

chapter one: february

february is slow
i detach myself from the darkness
that has pinned me here
i am slowly beginning to feel less numb
warmth and affection
seep back into my fingers and toes
i am feeling again
it starts with listening to music
i have always loved
and eating food
i always used to crave
but i proceed slowly
so that i do not take this joy for granted.

i laugh now
at the ridiculous concept
of you and me
a complex experiment
gone horribly wrong
but still
i tried
and there was a version of me
who would have blown up her entire life
just to have you spare her a glance
but now
i would not recognize that girl
even if she was standing
right in front of me.

i force myself into the waiting room
my mother and sister in tow
we are a team
leading the charge
and i thought i had armed myself
i thought i was steady
but soon the flood gates open
and i am no longer at the steering wheel
the tears are inevitable
and i have to let them be
because even this
this teary-eyed
twenty four year old woman
who wants to travel the world on her own
but cannot speak to the gynecologist
who cannot get a pap smear today
who feels embarrassment and shame
who grips tightly onto her mother's hand
even this woman
is still healing
and i ought to cut her some slack.

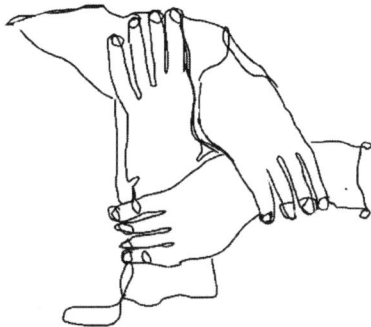

it has always felt like an impossible task
a chore that i never wanted to tackle
to express my needs
to friends
family
in relationships
as a woman
i never wanted to seem high-maintenance
and by never asking for anything
i thought i was self sufficient
a one woman show
creating her own natural resources
out of thin air
but i began to place
such a heavy burden on myself
because i thought
i was the only one capable
of carrying this weight
but it turns out
asking other people for help
telling other people what i need
does not make me weak
it makes me human.

trigger warning for the next page: suicide

we sit high in the sky
coasting above the clouds
but then the sky darkened
and life lost all of its light
in one moment
in an airplane bathroom
a man wrapped his belt around his neck
and hung himself from the ceiling
i can still see it so clearly
his friend desperately pounding the door
trying to punch his way in
there is an opening
and then chaos
a pale and still body
falls out of the bathroom
and a complete breakdown of society takes place
in fifty meters of space
a flash of scissors
a knife
they rush to cut his shirt down the middle
over an hour they work on him
i shrink into my seat
wrench my eyes closed
but even without my sight
i cannot disappear
a haphazard team
of nurses flight attendants anesthesiologists
start up a machine
place two pads on his chest
but nothing
and there on the floor of the aircraft
he chose to say goodbye to this world
and i find myself grieving for someone
i have never met.

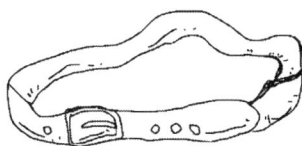

it feels odd
to only be present
for someone's darkest moment
someone who had an entire life
but i never saw it
i never saw him laugh
or smile
celebrate a birthday
or hug a loved one
i just have this one memory
this isolated image.

i want him to leave me alone
i do not need a reminder
of what will never be
do you not see
you have overstayed your welcome here
and i am ready for you to leave
but we have not talked in ages
and you have been gone a long time.

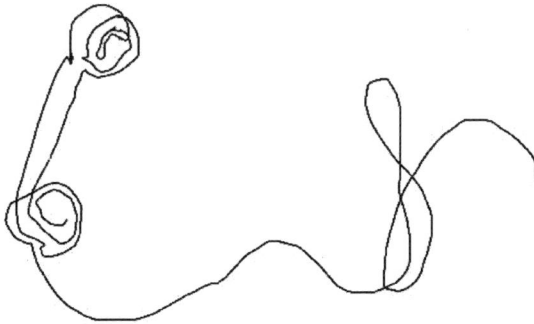

everything feels weighed down
my head
my eyes
my heart
that once had no limit
in what it could feel
now only feels cold and numb
this feeling
this emptiness
i find so difficult to describe
i go for a run
i eat a balanced diet
i write about how i am feeling
i talk to my therapist
and still
i am empty.

my eyes are tired
they crave rest
my brain has been overworked
and needs to be powered down
yet sleep does not come
my heart races too furiously
irrational thoughts plaguing my mind
i begin to think of the mistakes i have made
one month ago
one year ago
five years ago
ten years ago
before i know it
three hours have passed
three hours wasted on past mistakes
that i should not ruminate over
in the middle of the night
not when i have already identified
the lessons i need to take from them.

i grew up
not wanting the world to see my body
or my face
i wanted them to see inside of me
my values
and what i hold dear
what brings me to tears
and to laughter
but no matter how hard i tried
to push this narrative
they only saw
what they could take from me.

trigger warning for the next page: molestation

i am horizontal
my feet cannot reach the end of the table
my pants are off
fingers
invade places
they were never invited to enter
but i was so young
and these fingers
had more authority over me
so i let them be
because i was supposed to trust you
and i thought it was okay
but it turns out
the smile you wore
was only masking
a monster.

trigger warning for the next page: molestation

molestation
this word
is so ugly
and for so long
it has made me cringe
with uneasiness
humiliation
and shame
so i keep forcing myself
to use this word
molestation
more than i would like to
so that one day
i take back this word
and the power that was taken from me
and make it mine.

was this all i was missing
this small but invaluable blue pill
that restarted my heart
recaptured my spirit
made me feel again
love
anger
sadness
loss
joy
miraculous blue pill
we have started this sacred partnership
and so far
you have kept your promise
in bringing color back into my world.

i have always carried my tears
like heavy weights on my shoulders
and the world made me feel
like i was too sensitive
and i felt so much shame
because crying came so easily to me
and i have spent every day
resisting this part of myself.

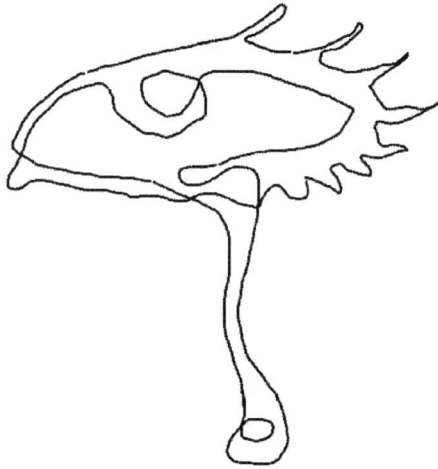

clothes that hide me
no make up
my hair always pulled back
or covering my face
avoiding contact with their wandering eyes
it seems my baggy clothes
cannot make me disappear
no matter how badly i want to
but they do prevent those eyes
from becoming hands
and this is good enough for now
i was twelve years old
and this was how i survived.

i want to forgive
i want to understand
i do not want to hate anyone
or feel like i can never trust again
but how does one forgive
something that seems unforgivable
and maybe i do not have to offer forgiveness
instead it is the submissive woman in me
that feels this nagging need
to offer forgiveness
who wants to take away his pain
when maybe the pain needs to be felt
by the man who caused it
in heaps and bounds.

i think back
to a time
where i truly felt like a child
and how quickly that changed
suddenly
my body was being looked at
reviewed by
more closely than ever before
and with less gentle eyes
these eyes now wanted something from me
when i was younger
i could not understand what they wanted
and now that i am older
i find it impossible to ignore
the motivation behind their gazes.

i have been wrong
so many times
that it makes me want to stop everything
so that i do not have to be wrong again
because getting it wrong
is energy stealing
and finding the lesson
in that wrong doing
is exhausting
but if i choose to live
with the fear of getting it wrong
keeping me from getting it right
i will choose to live a false life
and so i will swallow my pride
and the bitterness sitting on my tongue
and keep getting it wrong
and most definitely saying sorry
a couple hundred more times.

you are never too shy
to ask the wrong question
or say the wrong thing
you do not insist to know
something you do not know
you practice self awareness
the art of humbling yourself
to embrace the fact
that you cannot know all things
you are unshakeable
and would rather the world adjust to you
than for you to adjust to the world
an example of true courage
could you lend me some.

on the first day of high school
i was plucked out of my seat
in an auditorium
in front of all of my classmates
and told to follow a man
into his office
where he proceeded to tell me
that my shorts were too short
you made me cry in your office
and then showed me no empathy
you made me feel
like i had committed a heinous crime
that i could never make amends for
you made me call my mom
and interrupt her day
so that she could bring me
a change of clothes
you shamed me for the way
i dressed that day
when the only person
who should have felt shame
in that moment
is you.

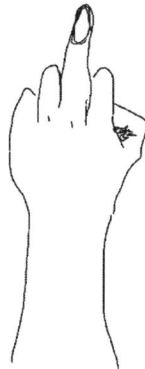

you are and can be all things
when i try to put you into words
i am reminded
that you are made up of infinite complexities
you can be caring and combative
determined and restless
hilarious and stoic
loud and quiet
selfish and selfless
open and private
gentle and tough
bold and restrained
and on and on and on
because the truth is
you are ever changing
and multi-dimensional
and this is the real human experience
a continuous contradiction of oneself.

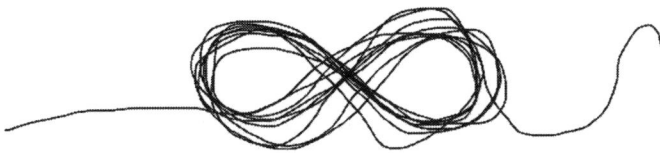

my dad
has never been afraid to cry
has never felt the need
to hide his tears
from me
from our family
from the world
he has always shed them
with confidence
in who he is
he does not see his tears
as a threat
to his masculinity
success
or status
he was the first to show me
that it is okay
for men to cry
in fact
it is normal
in my eyes
that is a real man
because that is human.

i religiously swallow a blue pill
and go for a run
and this is how i keep my head
without them
i wake up with my head on backwards
and my mind in disarray
it is a delicate system
keeping this head on straight.

i shoved my anger inside my closet
so far down
until it could not be seen
buried ten feet underground
i slammed the door closed
and by the time i let it rise to the surface
it almost blinded me.

there are times
where i want to recognize
that something is a universal experience
and other times
where i want that experience
to only be known by me
and feel the uniqueness
that comes from thinking
you are going through something
completely on your own.

stolen clothes
unruly laughter
making an appearance
in the darkest of times
a roll of the eyes
love void of conditions
scars that compliment one another
understanding without words
a friendship that will transcend time
my dear sister
this world would be colorless
in the absence of you.

chapter two: march

march
the month of intoxicating first times
of i don't know's
and where do i go's
the questioning of everything
if i can really do
what i said i will do
march proved to me
that i could.

thailand
my first destination
but certainly not my last
organized chaos
squares up to me on every street
a perpetual state
of perspiration and disorientation
but i don't mind
i don't want to be anywhere else.

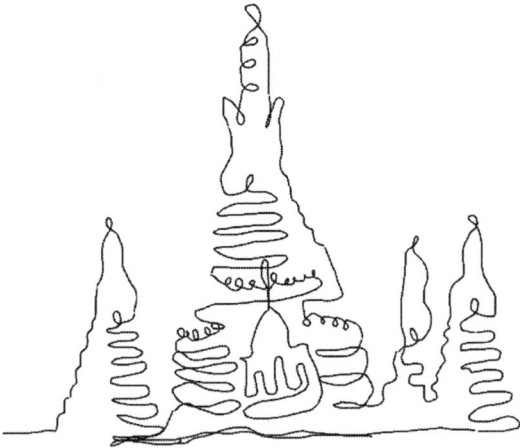

i stretch my hands up
and turn to face the sun
imploring it to swallow me whole
to wrap me in its warm embrace
light slips through the cracks between my fingers
and i welcome the glare
that casts down onto my face
i feel all of my muscles exhale
as if they have also been waiting for this moment
our first meeting with the sun
since winter.

as a little girl
there were times
i desperately wished
i was born a boy
anything but a girl
because to be a girl
was to feel a lack of control
was to have no sovereignty
in my own country
because to be a girl
was to have decisions made for me
a relentless supervisor
micro managing every step i made
was to feel like being pretty was my only option
a gentle and agreeable nature was required
any other adjectives were irrelevant
and so i quieted those parts of myself
that they did not approve of
to make them more comfortable
to avoid their ignorant line of questioning
but my rage is still here
it has always been here
simmering
just beneath the surface.

i did not want to make a splash
or draw attention
so i sat on the shore
where the water meets the sand
gazing at the water in longing
but refusing to take the plunge
so i am making up for lost time.

i used to have to force myself
to not think of you
and wish you the best
and it was exhausting
but now
you barely cross my mind
and if you do
i embrace it
because i have come to terms with
and have forgiven
all of the bad
including my own faults
in our messy ending
and now i only make space
for the good parts
and this is how i want to remember us.

old and gray
white men
young and beautiful
thai women
they intermingle in ways
that make my stomach
twist and turn
and i feel sick
that i was born
into this life
with so much opportunity
while so many of these women
are forced into this desperate situation
to satisfy
to fall to their knees
and bend into a fantasy
constructed by men.

i observe men
lurking in the shadows
and lurking in the open
they hobble down side streets
free to take advantage
of the economical situation
that has tied these women's hands
behind their backs
they do not want
to ride your decrepit cock
to earn a living
they need to
it is their survival
and you are their masters
maybe you think no one is watching
but i am watching
and now that my eyes are open
i refuse to close them again
i promise to stare and cast daggers
until you are the first to look away.

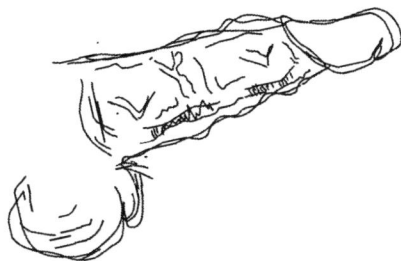

you
you with your foreign dollars
white face
and sense of entitlement
you
you with your mask of sophistication
arrogance
and ignorance
you ignore your conscience
screaming at you
that this is wrong
does it keep you up at night
knowing that you have bought sex
from a girl half your age
or younger
a daughter
a neice
a granddaughter
do you have enough power now
or will you never reach satisfaction.

look at me again
come a bit closer
and with a snap of my fingers
i will make you disappear
never to be seen again
people will ask what happened
and i will say
i have no clue
i was not there
with my fingers
crossed behind my back.

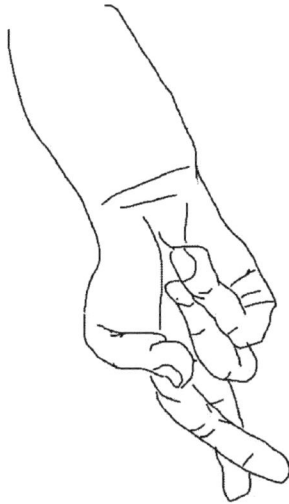

one day
one day this will come back to haunt you
and on that day
my body will be turned toward the sun
humming
and laying in the arms
of a beautiful man
who sees more
than just a body
and that is more
than i can say for you.

i feel like i am experiencing the world
for the first time
i do not know where i was before
but i only lived in the gray
and now i see
with every shade of the rainbow
available to me.

i tentatively *tap tap tap*
with the tip of my finger
i nudge and poke
but this is not enough
before today
i did not know
what my own clitoris looked like
and it is not as scary
as i thought it would be
i push a bit harder with my middle finger
and i start to feel like a total idiot
when i still feel no sensation
then
i move my fingers
in a circular motion
clockwise
and think *oh*
this is what everyone
is whispering about
i was twenty-two years old
experiencing pleasure
my first orgasm
induced by my own two fingers
for the first time.

twenty two years
of ignoring my body
of hiding from myself
and the most delicate parts of me
i was completely in the dark
unaware of the control i had
in creating my own pleasure
too terrified
to even consider the possibility.

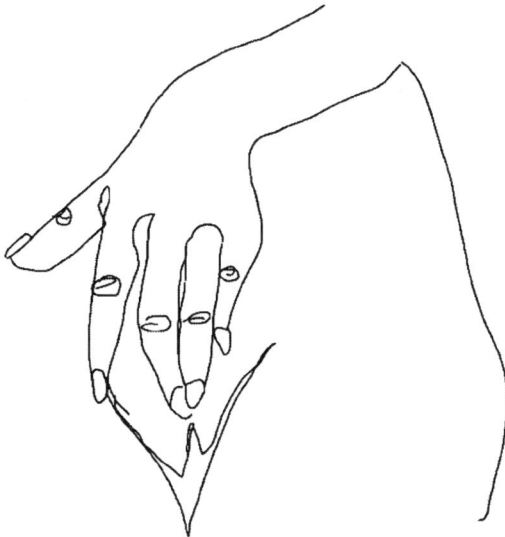

chapter three: april

april appears so abruptly
i barely catch its arrival
because of the distraction brought by march
this is the month of real healing
of conquering what i once thought impossible
and stepping through it
with honesty
power
grace
humor
and strength.

trigger warning for the next page: sexual assault

he is wearing a name tag
as an employee of this bus station
in the bustling city of hanoi
i ask him where the nearest atm is
he points to across the street
and then says he will show me
we cross the street
in the middle of the city
in a crowd of people
and in that moment
he decides to grab push force
his lips against mine
his hand travels down
to confidently squeeze my ass
as if my body has always been his
and has only been on loan to me
his friends are suddenly there
encircling the two of us
they are a pack of predators
building a barrier
because they had an alliance
long before me
and i was always going to be the prey
someone is recording
not wanting to miss
this prime opportunity
to capture the entertainment
they have front row seats to my nightmare
and their daydream
and i keep trying
to force my hands in between
to create space

(continues on next page)

but somehow
the space grows smaller
and i do not want to make them angry
or make things worse
but he forces his lips on mine again
and my rage
makes me feel capable of murder
they laugh
in the face of my rage
the funniest joke
they have ever heard
and all of a sudden they are gone
and i sit in the corner of the bus station
as my body tries to make itself disappear.

i am so angry
i am so angry that i start to cry
tears of red
with fire in my eyes
and every time i talk
lava pours from my mouth
do not ask me to calm down
to relax
or take a deep breath
because i am done being nice
i want to be angry
so let me be angry
let women be angry
for once
and do not blame me for my anger
blame yourselves
because you are responsible
it is you
who has subjected me to this rage.

you take this rage out of context
to prove your false innocence
resort to calling us crazy
and high-maintenance
emotional
high strung
bossy
a bitch
annoying
sensitive
all of which you say are reasons why
women should not lead towns cities countries
but the more i witness
women all around me
endure this suffering
the more of a necessity i see
for more women to become leaders
since men have already attempted the job
so many times
and have only engulfed the world in flames
that rise higher
with each passing day.

i make a promise to myself
that next time
i will not show mercy
they do not deserve my kindness
or sweet nature
they deserve the destruction
i would cause
with all of this anger
swelling inside of me.

i don't remember when i stopped raising my hand
but i was young
eight or nine
maybe younger
but it matters
that i stopped
because i have struggled to raise my hand
ever since.

the streets wind around me
presenting a risk at every turn
i am side stepping semi trucks
trying to not lift my foot off the gas
and train my eyes on the road in front of me
but the surrounding landscape whispers to me
take a look
and i turn my head
just for a second
and in that second
i take in the towering mountains
and deep valleys settled in between
in all of their grandeur
i have made it
to northern vietnam
i am driving a motorbike
and i have never felt this cool.

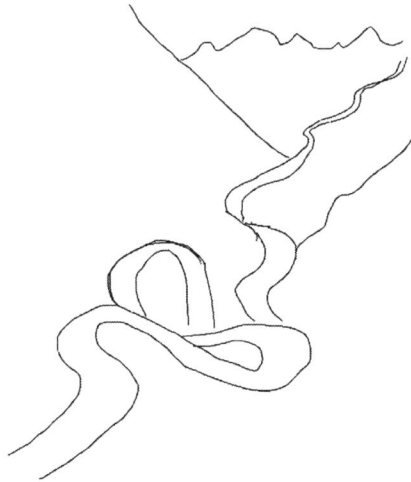

twenty four hours in singapore
that is all we were given
but with twenty four hours
we did not waste time
with four energy drinks consumed
and no sleep
twenty four hours
was more than enough time.

i look back on that night
with so much joy
because i was so sure of myself
and ready
and i had waited for so long
and suddenly the time had arrived
and i did not have time to shave my legs
or moisturize every inch of my skin
i did not reapply deodorant
or wear sexy lingerie
like i thought i would
instead i was a spontaneous explorer
uncovering new worlds
in a fancy hotel room
in singapore.

i was living in the dark
completely unaware
it could feel good the first time
my mind had prepared me for defeat
for blood pain and carnage
for tears and rejection
no one prepared me to feel pleasure
to feel joy
and light
and happy
and powerful
and isn't that how we should strive
for all women to feel
why do we prepare women
for pain and suffering
when this does not have to be our reality
let us change the narrative
yell from the rooftops
put up billboards
and air tv ads
prioritizing female pleasure
instead of treating it like a burden
let us make it the main attraction.

when i was young
i was made to believe
that the first man i had sex with
i had to be madly in love with
undeniably committed to
and preferably marry one day
and that all sounded logical
rational
until now
because now i realize
that i did not feel
this overwhelming urge
to desperately hold onto him
to follow him
to the end of the earth
actually
i was okay with letting him go
and found excitement
in exploring this brand new world
that had opened up to me
a world i never thought
i would have the password to.

i walk slowly up and down these streets
with my headphones in
i am in no rush
and i walk in no particular direction
singapore surrounds me
and i have never felt so confident
so sure
in a place that is brand new
trees intertwine with skyscrapers
two opposite worlds become one
people converge
from every corner of the earth
and cultures collide with one another
forming an alliance
sharing faith smiles food and celebrations
and for three weeks
i get to be a part of this.

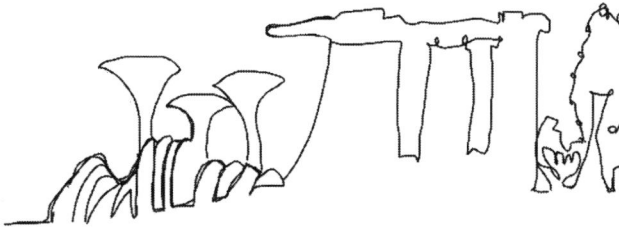

i recently turned twenty five
and i had lived in fear
of what i did not know
of the unfamiliar
for as long as i could remember
and then once it happened
i was set free
because i realized it can be beautiful
and pleasurable
but how could i know this
when there is such intensity
placed on a woman's first time
all of this unbearable pressure
to pick the right person
at the right time
to not be too young
or too old
and you can be excited
but not eager
there are all of these unspoken rules
but the truth is
it is all bullshit
because although sex is an act
experienced by many
it is also very personal
yet
like with everything in life
we try to paint it black and white
a one size fits all
but every woman is different
and so is every man.

i am learning
i am learning that it is okay to say no
to assert myself
in order to honor myself
you do not always have to be something
for someone else
sometimes
you can just be you
for you.

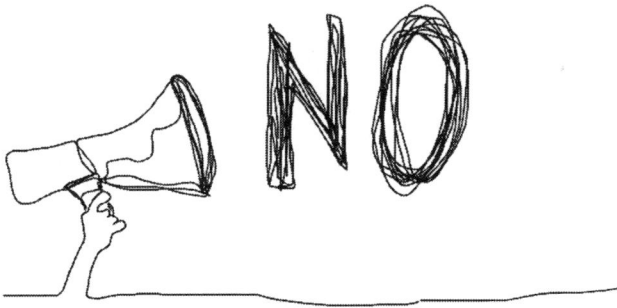

i have always rejected
the feminine parts of me
the parts i feared
would be relentlessly objectified
by those
who have no business
objectifying me
i would say
no no no i am not a girly girl
and fiercely rebelled against make-up
and tight clothes
as if to emphasize to people
with a neon sign:
no i am not a real girl
not one that you can peel with your eyes
or mock for her sensitivity and empathy
but i am ready to declare proudly now
that *i am a woman*
and i am embracing my femininity
and all of the beautiful scary and sad parts
that come with it.

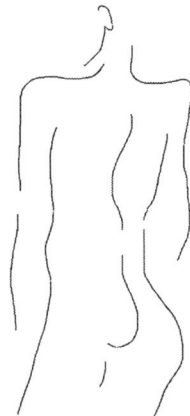

no one ever talked to me about sex
not in the way i needed them to
it was always a very methodical conversation
academic and without feeling
but sex is all about feeling
and how are women supposed to find pleasure
if no one wants to have a conversation
about how
how can i touch myself
how can i reach an orgasm
by myself
or with a partner
these questions bring us such discomfort
and ask yourselves why
why do we think ourselves
so undeserving of pleasure
that we cannot bear to voice these questions.

i never imagined
it could feel this good
a strength and willingness
to heal
coming directly
from within me
no one else
just me.

chapter four: may

may
may is partaking in late night excursions
consuming an excessive amount
of rum and cokes
making out
in the middle of deserted roads
and laughing the most
at our own jokes
may was waking up every morning
wondering where we would go
if we would kiss today
or not
it turns out
may
was just the beginning.

i have scooped ice cream
i have cared for children
changing diapers
wiping up vomit
employing every tactic
in the book of persuasion
to get them to eat or sleep
until i love them
like they are my own
i have carried expensive dinner plates
and cleaned off tables
with half eaten meals left behind
i have interned for a senator
only to realize
it is an unfeeling world
that i do not need approval from
nor need to be a part of
i have answered calls
from disgruntled clients
i have unclogged toilets
stripped dirty bed sheets
folded another's underwear
i have taught english
to people halfway across the world
and i have written reviews
for other peoples' words
and i know better now
than to try to predict
what i will do next.

in classrooms
we tell children
that their interpretation is wrong
and we shoot down their creativity
before they are old enough to drive
we push technicalities
and rubrics
we ask them to think outside of the box
and then lecture them
on the importance
of coloring inside the lines
so they go into the world
and see in black and white
when they have the potential
to build their own world
in technicolor.

he combs through my hair
analyzing judging measuring
he brings me over to a sink
i lay my head back
my eyes close on their own accord
they have been here before
they recognize this place
warm water caresses my scalp
fingers untangle my hair
until the knots come out
soap suds form
as shampoo makes its way to every strand
no piece is left behind
he is thorough and slow
he must know how good it feels
and for some reason
this stranger washing my hair
feels so much better than my own two hands.

it feels like the wind
is carrying me on its back
but there is no railing to grip
no rope to tie me down
and i am scared i will blow away
too far from who i was
and not end up
at who i want to be.

sometimes
my personality
decides to take some time off
because it is tired of being overworked
and only making minimum wage
so for one two several days
i forget who i am
operating on a low functioning generator
during a record setting snowstorm
but then
i meet someone who reminds me
of everything that is special
about the world
about the present
about me
and my personality rears its beautiful ridiculous head
and i am so relieved to see it again.

we duck under the waves
the skies darkening with each new cloud
thunder detonates in the distance
and our shoulders shake
with fear
and then laughter
with smiles so wide
we could swallow the whole ocean
and i don't remember when it happened
but i really want to kiss you.

we move through the countryside
at the speed of light
catching sight of lush greenery
that only the philippines
can provide
my arms are wrapped around you
my hands rest on your stomach
i let one finger circle your belly button
your stomach clenches
my cheek kisses your back
i feel you smile
and it feels too easy
that i could just lean down
and kiss the back of your neck
that i have been admiring
for over an hour
i don't
not now
but i will.

his fingers tread
like feathers over my stomach
his tongue
works its way around my nipple
one hand south
one hand north
i lose track
my sense of direction nonexistent
he warms me up
and my body readies itself.

chapter five: june

june
june is making plans
to see you again
because i cannot help myself
june is constant jet lag and stimulation
music festivals weddings and hot air balloon rides
the month of creating new friendships
and reuniting with old ones.

coming back home
after being away
i feel disoriented
i want people to see how i have changed
what i have experienced
do i not look cooler
older
wiser
but their eyes only allow them to see
the girl they grew up with
and i understand this
this wanting someone
to still feel familiar to you
but this girl
now feels like a distant cousin to me
a reoccurring role
that i still have to play.

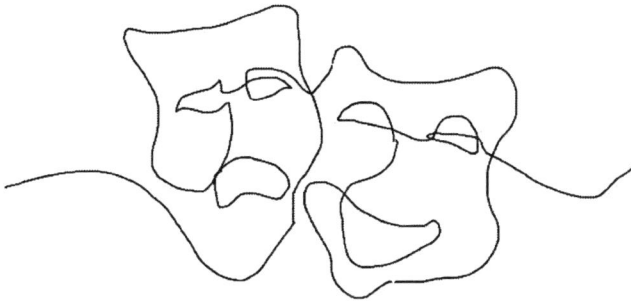

maybe we do not become best friends
but there is an unspoken truce
did one of us change
or was it the passing of time
there is no getting even
or sizing up
there are only small smiles
an occasional hello
and mostly silence
which feels so nice on my ears
so maybe it is not enemies to friends
but enemies to understanding
and i am grateful for this evolution.

men call out to me from their posts
that accompany every stall lining these streets
some of it makes my skin crawl
some of it makes me laugh
some of it i find completely ridiculous
and some of it i can understand
the sweet smell of traditional turkish coffee
entices me at every corner
my eyes are drawn to a rainbow of spices
which are the main attraction
displayed with intention and care
people squeeze by me
brush their shoulders with mine
and it is sensory overload
istanbul
you are an entire world
within one city.

blood stains hair vomit semen sand dust dirt beer wine
they confront it all
with grace and humility
a job
with no reward glamor or thank you
this is not a job
that is sought after
but still
they do it
heaving piles of dirty laundry
up and over their shoulders
like professional linebackers
they are scared of nothing
no one
they move in the background
quickly and quietly
and then the day is over
and they go home
only to return the next morning
to do it all over again.

when does the child leave us
and how do we earn their trust back
is it a permanent loss for some people
and a reoccurring annoyance for others
is it something to celebrate
or something to avoid
if you have lost your ability
to see the magic in the world
then i plead with you
to reintroduce yourself
to the child you left behind
to resume that lifelong friendship
because they will always remind us
of the beauty
that sits right in front of our eyes.

every sunday
my family would pack up our car
and drive to the beach
and friends and family would come together
forming one big group
and one sunday
a tall beautiful woman approached the group
and all the women started to huddle together
and whisper
they passed judgements on her
based on their own jealousy and insecurity
prosecution before any conversation
and my mom said to me
true confidence
is learning how to appreciate another's beauty
without seeing it
as a threat to your own.

it is easy to forget
that our youthful faces
with no signs of wrinkles marks or scars
are temporary
their expiration date
is inevitable
young faces will fade
into old
we have no control over these changes
and this lack of control
pushes us to look for solutions
to a problem
that is not a problem at all
but an inescapable result of living
and yet we panic
running to the closest product or service
that promises us the quickest relief.

i have witnessed mothers
absolutely abandon themselves
for their children
losing their happiness
to see to their child's
and it is so clear to me
that we need to take
better care of
our mothers
and prioritize them
being gatekeepers
to their own happiness
instead of being slaves
to our own.

so often
women have to cover their anger
with understanding
compassion
and a gentle embrace
but i want to pull the curtain back
and release this anger
so we do not have to hold it in anymore.

is it my never ending desire
for control
that i think myself so powerful
and capable
in shaping other's thoughts about me
it sounds irrational
when i put it into writing
but too often
i focus all of my energy
into creating an insurance policy
so no one will ever have a reason
to dislike me
i cross my own boundaries
say things i do not mean
and tread on their waters
to fulfill my insatiable ego.

chapter six: july

july
july is warm
it feels like biting into a soft banana pancake
drizzled with honey
it dissolves in my mouth
i try to savor it
to make it last
but eventually
i have to finish the pancake
and soon
i will long
for another one.

my legs nervously bounce up and down
my neck sore
from trying to sleep at an impossible angle
the plane's engine roars through my ears
i have not slept
i am too nervous
nervous
that i will not feel the same
or he will be disappointed
or that this connection
will have slipped away within the past month
but then the plane lands
i restlessly move through immigration
and baggage claim
i think people are walking slower than they have to
can they not recognize that i am in a hurry
and then i see you
and you smile so big
it lights me up
and suddenly i feel stupid
for feeling nervous at all.

i have departed this earth
touching down on an unfamiliar planet
i am not entirely sure where i am
but i feel comfortable and nervous
it is this all-encompassing feeling
that i have never known
he makes love to me
and each time a new part of me is unfastened
like a ball of yarn
i am *unraveling*
and the world gets
a little bigger.

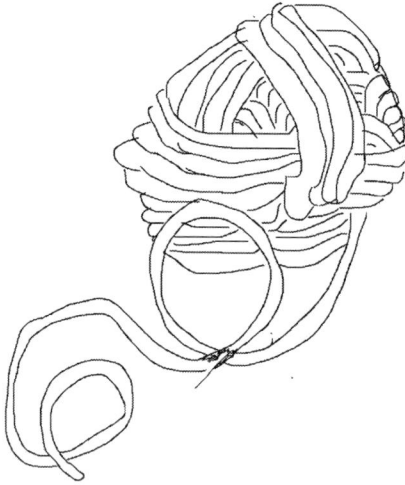

how long will this last
this laughing smiling looking feeling
the unsteadiness that comes
with something recently discovered
a surprise lathered in butter
this fleeting but perfect moment with you.

ten hours
is how long you drove
in one day
to show me the swiss alps
we napped at a gas station
at one in the morning
so you would not fall asleep
and on that drive home
where we were both delirious
with a combination
of happiness and exhaustion
something changed for me
and i started to look at you differently
i knew then
while we were winding around narrow roads
that hovered over cliffs
this would not be the last time
we would be together
and i was right.

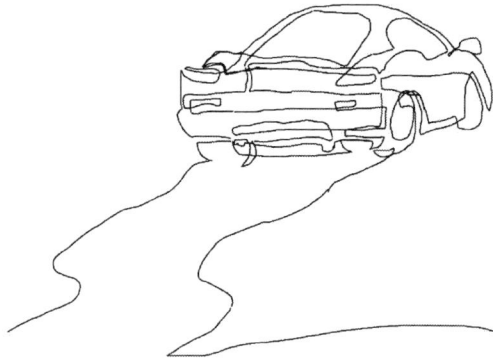

you are everywhere
my body my mind my fingers and toes
my lips my laugh my smile
the skin that creases around my eyes
behind my eyelids as i drift into a dream
i find you there.

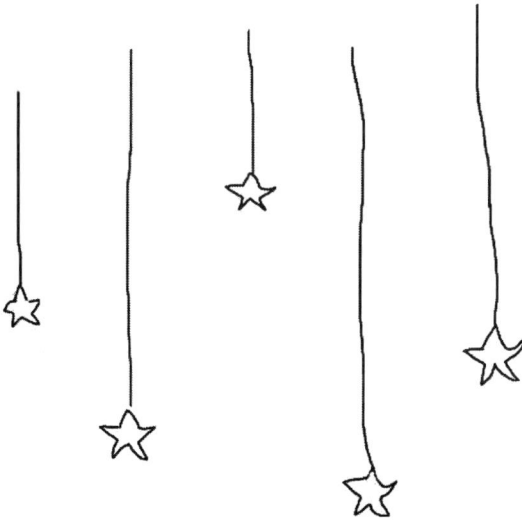

in many ways
i have been content with this day
i have made conversation with strangers
i have laughed
and i have smiled
yet my head is full of you
my mind will not let me forget
what you smell like
taste like
fuck like
remember when you said
you wanted more time
i think i want that too.

i had to leave
and i hate that i had to
the train pulled out of the station
taking me further and further away from you
but i knew i had to leave
because this is special
and i do not want to smother it
it must be met with patience and restrain
so i sit on this rooftop
so grateful for this view
but still covered in you.

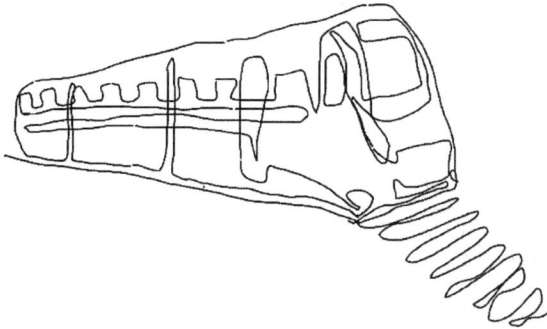

have you ever noticed how fast the clouds pass by
rushing to their next destination
they do not have a second to waste
and it is a reminder
of the continuous passage of time
that we so easily distract ourselves from
but then you are moving slow enough
to see the clouds
pass by above you
and realize time is always passing
whether you notice it or not
every second
every moment
onto the next.

the idea
of me hiking alone
for two weeks
in a foreign country
filled me with fear
so i knew i had to do it
and now that i have started
up and down these mountains
through the forest
alongside pastures
sitting in the german countryside
surrounded by no one
but my thoughts
the trees
a few grazing cows and sheep
and the sound of my feet
moving forward
now that i know i can do this
i am never going to stop.

i miss the feeling of you inside of me
i never knew i could feel like this
sexy and sensual
desired
it feels like i will never have enough
and it is not just anyone i want
it's you.

i am in a new town
sweetened by flowers
growing on every window sill
and children racing down sidewalks
zipping by on their tricycles
they see who can reach the end of the street first
then argue about who won
and it is all so normal
so beautifully mundane
and what a privilege this is
to witness the mundane
of the day to day.

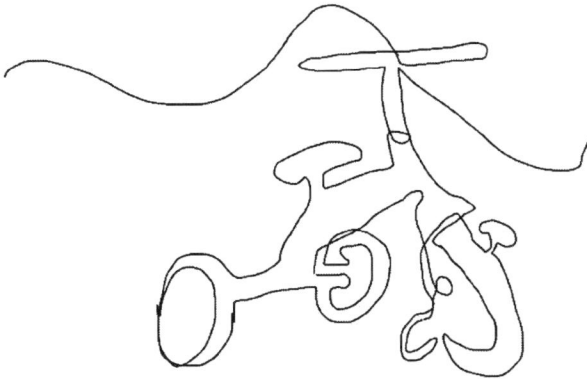

i wish i could have
a conversation with these trees
see what they have seen
feel what they have felt
some have been alive
for thousands of years
their branches swaying in the breeze
gathering years of ancient wisdom
the kind of wisdom
that can only be acquired
with the passing of time

i wake up early this morning
drink two cups of coffee
outside the air is cool
but it will turn by late morning
and the sun will revive me
i will walk to the market
try to speak a language i do not know
and i will feel judgmental eyes on me
but these stares cannot break my mood

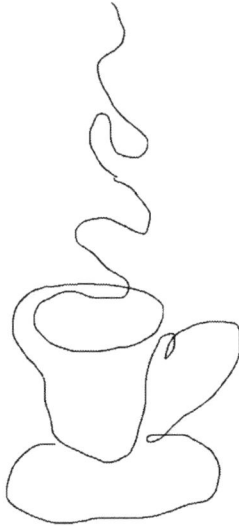

i have never known this with a man
this feeling of being myself
and that being enough
more than enough
i do not have to prove anything
or tiptoe around his ego
i am just able to be
and there has never been a sweeter peace than this.

when i am exhausted
i do not want to sleep
because when i am asleep
i cannot look at your face
hear your voice
or touch your hair
so i will stay awake
until sleep forces itself upon me.

his mouth
a mustache accompanied
by its own personality
eyes full of blue
and flecks of green
i lay with him
wake up next to him
make him laugh
watch him smoke his after dinner cigarette
the most ordinary of days with you
are extraordinary.

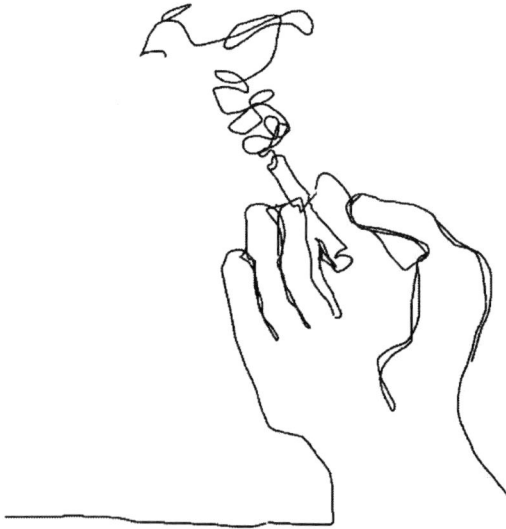

his fingers graze down my spine
the insides of my thighs
and my hand grips the back of his neck
pulling at the ends of his hair
we rub
caress scratch tug and sigh
never as close
as we aim to be
but we desperately try
as etta once sung
at last
suddenly i am singing too
and i finally understand what that song is about.

chapter seven: august

august passed slower
than any other month
it was a month of questioning
of doubts and uncertainty
of temptation and restrain
of venturing to deserted islands
and trekking up intimidating mountains
i will never forget august
and will always be thankful
that it introduced me to you.

i walk down the sidewalk
and try to look relaxed
but all i feel are eyes
and i am highly aware
of my womanhood
my face
my hair
my body
my femininity
i square my shoulders
narrow my eyes
and set my mouth
in a straight line
to try to look as unappealing as possible
i ignore their stares
they cross the sidewalk
and now they will be walking
straight past me
one hundred feet
fifty feet
twenty five
ten
three
two
one
they pass by me
and keep walking
still
i look behind me
because i can never be too careful
and i breathe a sigh of relief
when i only see their backs
walking further away from me.

it is constant movement
and awkward introductions
always meeting new people
and learning new names
i am starting to crave what is familiar
the familiarity that comes
with sitting in the silence
and dreading when i cannot.

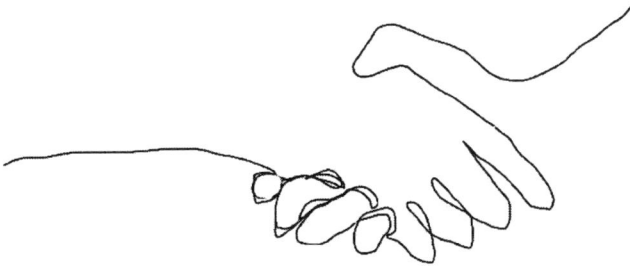

i give compliments
when i am feeling insecure
to stop the negative thoughts
in their tracks
and to stop the relentless voice scolding me
from inside of the mirror
a result of comparing myself
to beautiful women
from all around the world
i feel helplessly plain
i am not cool without effort
there is no sophisticated air about me
i am clumsy
a bit spacey
a pushover at times
who says sorry way too much
and cries way too easily
i wear my heart on my sleeve
for everyone to see
the opposite of a mystery
and i am working on loving
this version of me.

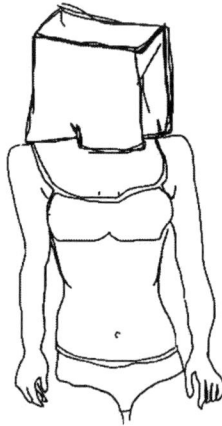

i feel like i am sixteen again
how do you know if someone likes you
sometimes the thought crosses my mind so loudly
i panic he will hear it
each conversation builds on the last
and the more i know
the more i want
i feel an overwhelming sense of urgency
to know every detail
every heartache
every flaw
every triumph
every mistake
give me everything
and i still won't be satisfied.

why do we trust certain people
but instinctively not others
is it something we perceive in their eyes
or an indecipherable energy
that passes between two people
this immediate trust disarms me
it is unexpected
in a world that conditions us
to see the worst in one another
but there is still time to trust
even if you are convinced
that all is lost.

we have trekked up to mount batur
an active volcano
sitting on the island of bali
and on the way down
a crowd of monkeys appear
and almost on instinct
people around me pull bananas out of their pockets
it is feeding time
and i ask myself
where would the monkeys be right now
if tourists did not feed them
drawing them back
to the same spot
every day
where were they
before we came
what did their days look like
and when did they start revolving around us.

cool blue eyes
a kind heart
the way you say *fuck*
your lips
and the way they feel against mine
these thoughts intrude
without asking for permission
and i am helpless
in preventing their arrival.

hardwood that creaks with the lightest step
the relentless sound of rain
instant coffee and banana pancakes
a mosquito net that has seen better days
the smell of smoke
a flash of green
a sea of blue
this will always remind me of you.

billie
my one hundred and three year old friend
wisps of white hair that floated in every direction
and the seriousness you brought
to every game of dominos
i still remember hearing the pride in your voice
each time you introduced me as your friend
no one has ever been that proud
to call me their friend
no one has ever loved me as quickly as you
and just as quickly as you loved me
time decided
that you had reached the end
and isn't this always the hurdle
a lack of time
but you did not feel it was too soon
you had lived
and felt ready to die
this resolve
this contentment and acceptance
with your own death
is the most generous way
you could have said goodbye to me
and to everyone who loved you.

these island skies are hostile
they show no mercy
releasing heavy rain
and damning thunder
the kind of rain
that makes me want to lose myself
in a book
or kiss a boy
either would do.

my body is levitating
i cannot remember
what i was doing before
or what i planned to do after
a thought comes to mind
that i might drift too far
and my body begins to tense
and sink
but then i allow the thought
to pass through me
and soon i am levitating again
barely touching the water
gently lifted up
and then brought back down
without so much as a sound
hands turned upward
palms facing the sky
and the warmth of the sun
on the surface of my skin
is such a nice contrast
to the cool waters beneath me.

conversations about death
and everything in between
past memories
meeting the present
 pushing me to talk
about her
about him
about me
you give me space
to talk about hard things.

point stare grab and grope
they take and take and take
until there is nothing left
they think they can go on in this way forever
but aren't you tired
isn't everyone so fucking exhausted
there must be an end
how do you help someone
who sees nothing wrong
they cannot feel our inner rage
only when it is their sister
mother
wife
daughter
only then
do they start to show concern
only then
do they start to listen
to what we have been screaming at the sky
since the start of time.

how long
how long have i been living with this fear
and when will it release me
or will it always be here
the harsh stares of men subdue me
a constant reminder of what could happen
so i make myself smaller
and try to take up less space
an anger so loud with nowhere to go
i do not want to be this angry
it is their burden and their burden alone.

it feels like i give a man an inch
and they assume the right
to dominate my world
they show me kindness
gift me with desserts coffee fresh flowers
gifts that i never asked for
in the first place
and all of a sudden the dynamic shifts
my naivety dissolves
and i understand the intention
behind these gifts
because now he supposes
i owe him something
or everything
and it seems futile
to try to discern the good from the bad
and i am tired of trying to see good
instead i just see a man
standing in front of me
like they have
so many times before
swearing they want nothing
while trapping me into a corner
and demanding everything.

it is more discouraging to know
this is not a singular experience
but one experienced
by almost every woman i have met
from the united states
to singapore turkey indonesia thailand
to spain germany vietnam and the philippines
i get to know these women
from all over the world
and in every conversation
a running theme of rage and discomfort
as we are confronted
by the misogyny
that lives at the center of our lives
no matter how hard
we try to fill the space around us
with love respect and human decency
we are still left with this reality.

why are we so afraid to say how we feel
do we not want to seem
like we care too much
instead we wait
we wait until we are gathered at a funeral
or until someone is walking away
and we bite our tongue
with what we wish we could say
but isn't that one of the greatest gifts
you could give to someone
to reveal what you see in them
and what they mean to you.

do you ever think about that one person
the one you were never quite sure about
that made you question everything
that made you feel seen
and heard
but it did not amount
to the fantasy
you constructed inside of your head
so you had to let them go
and try to forget
but still they remain
taking up space in your mind
you never were very good at saying goodbye.

i am starting to forget what you look like
and i have no picture to remind me
nothing but my own unreliable memory
and i feel desperate
so fucking desperate to hold onto you
in whatever way i can
but you are slipping away
and soon you will be gone
both of us longing for past days.

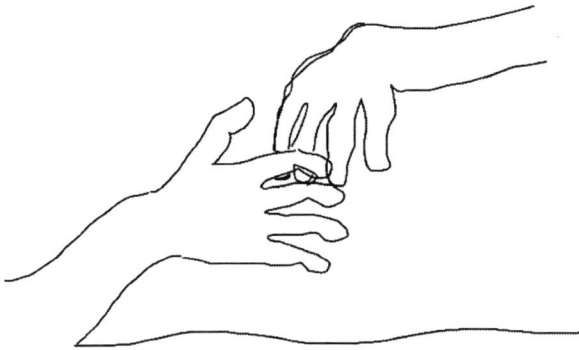

chapter eight: september

september
september intentionally draws attention to my fears
contributing to my increasingly convoluted mind
as october approaches
my insecurities take hold of me
withhold withdraw project
and i struggle to love these shadowy parts of myself
that need my love the most
but september
is about me setting those insecurities free
to make space for what is
this beautiful world
and you.

cobblestone streets
lined with cafes and ice cream
the young and old come together
their sounds of laughter fill the square
and this laughter fills me with warmth
i want to bottle this warmth
for days that i am lacking it.

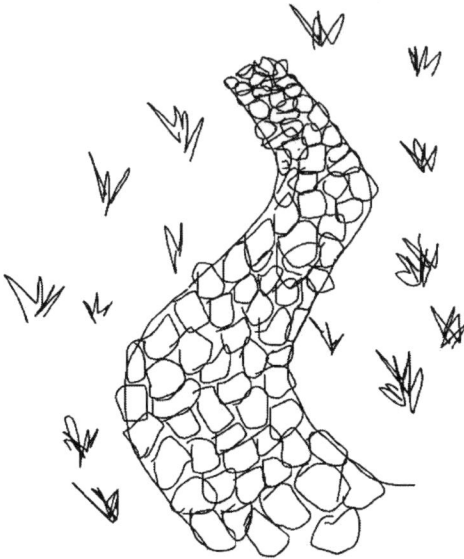

i sit
with your jacket on
sipping a tall glass of red wine
for as long
as the sun will let me
but the winter air is settling in
making itself at home
and i know these nights
sitting out here
in the open air
until dark
with the sound of laughter
spilling over
from next door
are in limited supply.

i thought i would be sure
about you
about us
but the time is approaching quickly
for me to know what i want
and i feel off balance
which is contradictory
to the steadiness i have felt
during these last four months with you.

all i can think about
is hurting you
before you can hurt me
why
why am i like this
when did this start
and how do i free myself
from this never ending cycle.

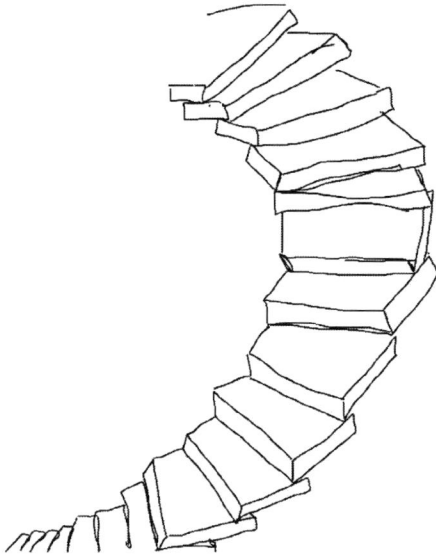

i need to keep learning
so that i can know better
i will do and say the wrong thing
but i will keep getting it wrong
so i can get closer to getting it right
and it is better to say the wrong thing
than to say nothing at all
there are far worse things
than being criticized
like being a coward.

working hard for what you want is important
but so are rest and stillness
your worth
is not married to your productivity
but to who you are as a whole
so let's stop
stop trying to prove how busy we are
to everyone
who makes us feel insecure
let's stop
making impossible to-do lists
and confining ourselves
to these superhuman expectations
because as much as you try to be
you are no superhero
so allow yourself to rest
without justification
just because.

i keep telling myself
that we are just having fun
we do not need to add weight
instead we can continue to laugh tease smile
but there is a depth to this
that i did not see at first
and now this depth is stalking me
sticking to me like a shadow
showing up out of the blue
and knocking on my front door
desperate for an invitation
to come inside
so i turn up the music
and cover my ears with my hands
but i cannot ignore this persistent knocking
growing louder every day
and i cannot silence it
no matter how hard i try.

i have known not caring enough
and caring too much
i have known a connection dissolving
before it has even begun
but i have never known this
this consistency
this trust and open communication
but still
i struggle to believe what you say
and fight to keep these self sabotaging thoughts
from overthrowing this harmony i feel.

it is not what i expected
there are no warring families
or someone forbidding our relationship
there is no yelling
and then sharing a heated kiss
instead
there is cooking meals
and washing dishes
sitting in the silence
and talking nonsense
pretending to be adults
in fancy hotel robes
laughing
until we need something to hold onto
there is miscommunication
frustration
honesty
an embrace
and then understanding
a never ending cycle
of learning
about one another
but i am willing to keep learning
to have these moments with you.

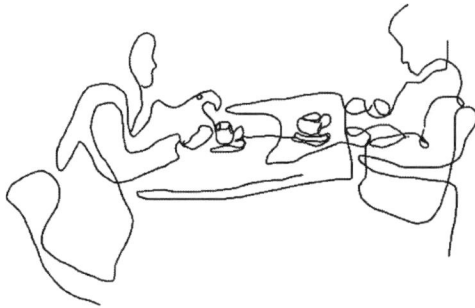

if you decide
to stop choosing me
it will hurt
for days weeks months
but i know i will be okay
because i have seen joy and suffering
and i know that joy is felt more deeply
after enduring pain.

i said *your eyes are blue*
you said mine are golden
but i know they have always been brown
and still you see golden
and i should have known then
but i didn't
and i almost let my insecurities
tear down everything
for nothing
but my own self preservation.

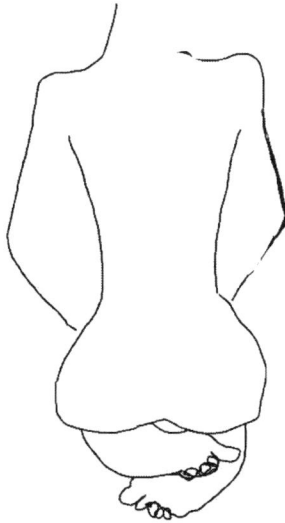

ten minutes
ten minutes infused with toxicity
they issue threats
masking their menace with smiles
the smell of alcohol
suffocating me
they speak with arrogance
sharp on their tongue
and people wonder
why i am without trust
and since you require a reason why
here it is
this predatory behavior
is a universal experience
all women have no choice
but to weather and tolerate
we did not ask for this
there is no sex appeal or arousal
resulting from your catcalls
and wandering hands
that move closer with the subtlety of a bulldozer
and i think it is time to dismantle the bulldozer
once and for all.

tread lightly
or i will prick you with a needle
when you are least expecting it
and pray that you never wake up
from the deepest sleep
or is that too kind
i am tired of showing mercy
to those who do not deserve it.

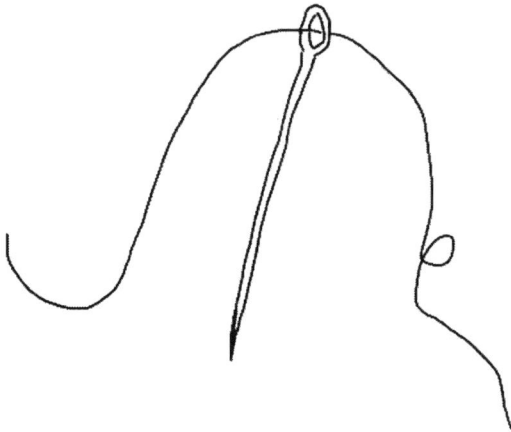

always in want
of something in return
is it genuine or calculated
because i never know
so i air on the side of caution
because my instincts
tend to be manipulated
and i have been fooled by your tricks before
unaware of your true motivations
so i will not offer smiles and kindness
if it means sacrificing my sense of security.

sleep is creeping closer
my eyes feel heavier
my breaths become deeper
and your voice cuts through the silence to say
i just want you to be so happy
and i believe you
more than i have ever believed any man
and i feel safe and cared for
and so grateful to lay in this bed beside you.

i often spent my nights day dreaming
too afraid
to dream during the day
playing a losing game of chicken
bordering between real and pretend
and i had become so familiar
with being on my own
but i had to make a choice
to live in the real
or to stay in this beautiful dreamland
but my mind could have never
crafted a dream like this
because this is too real
to qualify as a dream
it is something i can see hear smell touch taste
and with all of my senses activated
i am finally living in the present
and making a choice
has never been this easy.

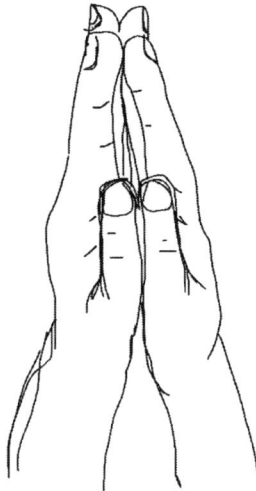

every time i have sex
i am overcome with gratitude
because there was a version of me
not too long ago
who thought she never would have sex
that kind of intimacy
and penetration
had frozen her with fear her whole life
and she could never imagine finding someone
she could trust enough
to completely let go
of those fears
and irrational thoughts
and then she met you
and your heart was so kind
and even though we have not talked in a while
i just want to say thank you.

thinking back
to last winter
i do not recognize that girl
because that girl
was so spooked by her own shadow
she could never walk in the sun
for fear of shining a spotlight
on the darkest parts of herself.

the air is colder
but the bed is getting warmer
and every time i smile
you smile too
and i am making a choice
to choose you
and in a way
i am choosing me too.

you saw qualities in me
that i had been waiting
for a man to catch sight of
and yes
there was a physical attraction
but you looked further
into the back of my mind
into the depth of my loving
and you saw me
the me that had felt
so irrelevant to men for so long
you drew light
to this version of me
arranged a celebration
and i never want
this party to end.

my anger and i
had become so estranged
and i thought we would never make amends
but then i learned
that my anger needed my love
just as much as my happy
and so now
anger and i
are becoming close friends.

home
home used to be a place
high school
and people i had grown up with
who knew me with braces and acne
and then home became the mountains
and retirement homes
with friends who will last a lifetime
and now
home is anywhere
i can be surrounded
by people i have never met
who speak a different language
i can shop at a new grocery store
and go on late afternoon walks
in a completely foreign neighborhood
and still call that place my home.

here i am
on my own again
but i am also with you
and it just so happens
i can commit to someone else
and also commit to myself
these two ideas
are not mutually exclusive
and after coming to this realization
life feels a lot less fucking lonely.

my journey with depression

During the winter of 2021 and heading into the year 2022, I was suffering from depression. It was one of the most intense feelings of emptiness and despair I had ever felt. It felt like it came out of nowhere. I had just moved into an airbnb in Pennsylvania and was living alone for the first time in a long time. It started with feeling like a failure every morning I woke up, with hours of crying during the day, and feeling increasingly more numb to everything around me. I tried to desperately cover these feelings with laughs and smiles, but they were only failed attempts to hide my depression from my closest friends and family. I had so much shame about not being able to handle daily life on my own, and a few weeks into having these feelings consistently, I started to have really scary thoughts about not wanting to live on this earth anymore. This was a wake up call for me. It was a sign that I needed to tell someone how I was feeling and I am so grateful that I did.

It started with calling my mom and dad and then confiding in my sister. We all decided it was best if I came back home for a while, until we were able to figure out what was going on internally. It seems like a miracle that I am now the happiest I have ever been. But it is not a miracle; it was several months of therapy, crippling self doubt, crying, feeling numb and empty, forcing myself to eat, dress, shower, exercise, journal, and talk to family and friends.

It was only when I started to take antidepressants that I finally started to feel like the me before the depression came. These pills saved my life, but I completely respect and understand that this is not the answer for everyone, but they are an option, and I want anyone struggling to know they have options. I feel so grateful that the first medication I tried worked for me because many people, including some of my best friends, struggle for years before finding what works for them and sometimes they never do. To anyone reading who is currently living with depression or another mental illness: you do not have to suffer in silence.

mental health resources

betterhelp.com

Better Help is a resource I have personally used to find affordable therapy during the darker seasons of my life. If anyone is even considering therapy as an option, Better Help is one of the most affordable ways I have found to find a licensed professional to talk to. We all need help sometimes and Better Help is paving the way for making therapy more accessible to all.

988 Suicide & Crisis Lifeline

Call or text 988 to connect with a professional crisis counselor.

Crisis Text Line

Text "HELLO" to 741741
This hotline is available 24/7 and also connects you with a professional crisis counselor who can provide you with more support and information.

https://www.nimh.nih.gov/health/publications/5-action-steps-for-helping-someone-in-emotional-pain

This link directs you to the National Institute of Mental Health's website, where they provide information on how to help someone in emotional pain.

Selfcare Space

This is an app that provides self-guided therapeutic programs for $18/month.

personal mental wellness

Disclaimer: I am <u>not</u> an expert in psychology. Below I have only listed practices that have proven to be successful in keeping my inner peace.

Sleep
It is much easier for me to be drawn toward a negative thought pattern or spiral when I am sleeping less. My mind is so much stronger when I acquire eight or nine hours of sleep every night. Sometimes this means saying no to things and letting certain people down, but I realized that I need to be okay with disappointing people if it means protecting my inner peace.

Exercise
Exercise can look differently for everyone. Personally, I have decided that running, long walks, stretching, and yoga all need to be a part of my daily routine. Not only do these exercises help me stay focused in the present, but they also help quiet all of the unnecessary noise and thoughts that threaten to disrupt my peace of mind.

Rest
It is really hard to allow yourself to rest without justification in a society that only values rest as a reward. But there are days when I wake up and I just don't feel like myself, and no matter what I do, I just feel off. On these days, I let myself decide what I want to do— whether this be not talking to anyone, laying in bed all day, or deleting the to-do list I made the night before. Sometimes rest for me can look like hours of sleep or taking a break from socialization by turning my phone off.

Journaling

It can be difficult to bring yourself to write about how badly you're feeling, especially when you are trying to distract yourself from those feelings. The feelings do not magically go away after I write them down, but writing about them helps me understand myself better, so I can recognize those feelings and thoughts that are not necessarily healthy for me in the future.

Journaling also lets me see on paper the way I am talking to myself in my head. I realized that I can be really mean and harsh and I talk to myself in ways I would never talk to another human being. Identifying this pattern allowed me to reverse these thoughts and make them more positive and constructive, and I started to talk to myself the way I try to talk to others—with kindness and understanding.

Mindfulness

For me, mindfulness is about keeping my mind in the present. It is about recognizing *the here and now*. I practice mindfulness through drawing, painting, cooking, active listening, writing, going for walks and noticing everything around me.

I also wanted to add an exercise that I was provided after going to therapy for a few months. It is an exercise I use when I am feeling especially overwhelmed, anxious, or just cannot seem to settle my inner thoughts, and it really helps me step back into my body. The exercise is called the 5-4-3-2-1 Technique:

What are five things you can see?
What are four things you can feel?
What are three things you can hear?
What are two things you can smell?
What is one thing you can taste?

Sometimes I like to close my eyes after the first question to really become aware of my other senses: touch, sound, smell, and taste. The aim of this exercise is to ground you—to place your mind back into the present moment.

Setting Boundaries

There are personal boundaries I have set with myself, such as only reading or watching the news in the morning but not before bed and saying '*no*' to making plans when I need to recharge my social battery alone. I still struggle with creating boundaries with friends, family, strangers, and even myself, but after reading 'The Book of Boundaries' by Melissa Urban, I am finding it easier to state my boundaries in a way that is clear and self-honoring. I highly recommend this book to anyone who struggles with being a chronic people pleaser, like myself.

special thank you

I want to thank one of my best friends, Meghan Rayhill, for contributing to the mental health resources I have included. Without her knowledge and willingness to show such vulnerability and transparency regarding her own mental health struggles, I could never be as honest as I have been in this book. I met Meghan when I was in college. During this time in my life, I was still getting used to the idea of being vulnerable, of confronting my own trauma, and being honest with myself and the people I love. Meghan showed me that my vulnerability was my strength, and without her embodying these words everyday, I never would have had the strength to share these words with the world. Meghan, thank you for your courage to be honest, even when it is hard.

about the author

Karli Crispin grew up in the small beach town of Lewes, Delaware. She moved away from home to attend James Madison University, where she earned a bachelors degree in International Affairs. She always dreamed of traveling the world and in March of 2022 she bought a one way ticket to Thailand, and started her journey of traveling to nine countries on her own. She has met some interesting characters along the way—some who have inspired the poems in this book. As an avid observer of the human experience, Karli's home changes from month to month as she searches for her next adventure; whether it be motorbiking in northern Vietnam or living on a deserted island off of the coast of Indonesia.

If you want a glimpse into Karli's world beyond the text, go to **http://karlicrispin.wixsite.com/karli-crispin**

Printed in Great Britain
by Amazon

50342616R00092